"Donabie skilfully b[...]ting the glorious majesty of Mother Earth against dire warnings of her peril. The poetry is lush, powerful, and compelling. Not only will you immerse in the beauty of the experience, but it will have you seeing and thinking about the world in new and wonderful ways. The stunning artwork and photography deepen the journey."

- Cindy Watson, award-winning and best-selling author of *The Art of Feminine Negotiation* and *Out of Darkness*.

"[A] beautiful, beautiful book. [Donabie's] poetry and pictures are both wistful and stunning."

– Lori Knowles, Editor, *Ski Canada Magazine* and author of *Summers with Miss Elizabeth*

"Exploring the central nervous system of our Mother Earth through Wendies poetic musings is guaranteed to ignite all five senses. Views from the Edge of the Earth transports the reader with each intimate musing."

– Paul Feist, author of *Broken Anchor*

"Reading Wendie's poetry and prose, we feel the words as they open like pearly *white petals. Both a soothing and prodigious experience. The combined emprise of the visual and interpretation of the text, is indeed a magical covenant. A vehement blend of urgency and hope."*

– David Bruce Patterson, author of *Square Wheels* and *Forthright But Furtive.*

"Tendrils of reverence entwine with joy, grace, and hopefulness. Find your own way back to Mother Earth and all she offers. Love large and dig deep into the reverent words and paintings. Be like Wendie, be present. Wendie's heartfelt words and captivating paintings will make your heart beat just a little faster. See your own colours in the black and white of this reverent book."

– Sheridan Rondeau. author of *Dear Braveheart A Caregiver's Loving Journey Through Alzheimer's Dementia*

Views from the Edge of the Earth

Poetic Reflections & Images

Wendie Donabie

W Donabie

Shani
Hope you enjoy my Views of our beautiful planet.
Wendie

Views from the Edge of the Earth is a collection of poetry, prose, and images by Wendie Donabie.

Published by
Heron's Nest Studio Press
95 Muskoka Road
Bracebridge, ON P1L 1H4

For more information and additional copies contact:

Heron's Nest Studio at the address noted above.

Second Edition 2025

ISBN 978-1-7383323-0-4

Printed concurrently in Canada by:

Marquis —A Division of Lakeside Book Company
Quebec, Canada
marquisbook.com

Cover Image: MOTHER EARTH – OUR SHARED ROOTS, Acrylic on Canvas.

Africa is considered the birthplace of humanity.

Dedicated to

Mother Earth

May you heal.

May you thrive.

May you continue

to teach us how to live.

Algonquin legend tells us,

"beneath the clouds lives the Earth—Mother from whom is derived the Water of Life, who at her bosom feeds plants, animals and humans"[1] She is also known as Nokomis, the Grandmother. The first Greek God was Gaia, or Mother Earth. *From her fertile womb all life sprang, and unto Mother Earth all living things must return after their allotted span of life is over.* [2]

1 Larousse 428). (8)

2 (Source From the website, greekmedicine.net)

Painting image: MOTHER EARTH - Our Shared Roots, AFRICA - The Cradle of Humanity, Acrylic on Canvas, ©Wendie Donabie.

Preface

Long ago, indigenous peoples developed a relationship of respect and interdependence with Mother Earth. They felt her rhythms, recognized her cycles, listened to her voice and learned from her. The rock taught them faith, wisdom, strength, and endurance while the trees illustrated honesty and uprightness. As the sap flowed through the trees, so must honesty flow through the people. When they trod upon the grass, it bounced back teaching them to be resilient, kind to themselves and others. Animals taught companionship, how to care for and protect one another.

Today, Mother Earth continues to share these lessons; she teaches us to be human. As her children, our job is simple: listen to her and care for her.

> When I walk through the forest, I feel her support beneath my feet as she responds to each footfall. *Feel me, touch me, embrace me*, she says.
>
> Her scent wafts through the air filling my nostrils with the living smells of the earth, water, and plant life. *Breathe deeply; fill your body, heart, and soul with my abundance*.
> From quiet lakes, gurgling brooks, rushing rivers, roaring waterfalls, and mighty oceans, I hear her enduring heartbeat. *We are one, each a part of one another. What affects one, affects all.*
>
> Her voice travels on the wind, through the calls of birds; I see her messages in the movement of wildlife and hear them echoing through her canyons and valleys. *Know me; know your brothers and sisters. Care*

for each other. Everything you need is here for you to use, not abuse.

This is my experience; it's a spiritual one. It's how I relate to Mother Earth. I feel her, hear her, and see her in every moment of my day. To me, she is the Mother of us all. However, just as each child relates in a different way to his or her own mother, your connection with Mother Earth will be unique. I encourage you to develop a relationship with her. She is a wise advisor and . . . we all need her.

Wallace Earle Stegner, American historian, novelist, short story writer, and environmentalist said, "*Something will have gone out of us as a people if we ever let the remaining wilderness be destroyed . . . so that [we] never again . . . see ourselves . . . [as] part of the environment of trees and rocks and soil, part of the natural world and competent to belong in it.*" [3]

∞

[3] https://www.wilderness.org/articles/article/wallace-stegner

Contents

Introduction

We live in a world of incredible beauty, remarkable in its biodiversity from microscopic to gigantic life. Yet, we're killing our planet with the waste and harm we've done — habitat lost, and species gone or fading fast.

Does this mark the end? Is it coming soon? Or will our great-grandchildren's future be cut short? Can we learn to share our resources and collaborate to find solutions? Do those who have the power to bring about change, care enough to act before it's too late? Or will we wipe out all life including ourselves?

The answers are out there. I believe we can still save the Earth.

∞

For some time, I have pondered our fate and our future, seeking a way to help, to give back—to leave behind something of value. That was my purpose in writing this book — to add my voice to those calling for action to protect and preserve this extraordinary planet we call home.

In *Views from the Edge of the Earth*, I share the beauty, the joy and, at times, the pain I experience in living every day. Written in a simple, straightforward style, the collection begins with a dire vision but ends with a message of hope. Some entries may cause you to think differently, others may simply bring a smile to your face. I hope you enjoy your reading journey.

A View from the Edge of the Earth

I see Hellfire rising
to embrace the follies of mankind,
a burning platter of human flesh
falling from Earth into the abyss.

Evil exists,
but only in the hearts and minds of the arrogant, the selfish.
No godlike being has condemned us,
we have done that ourselves.

What the world needs now is LOVE—
turning our thoughts outward
from our self-centred preoccupation.
Redemption? Is that possible?

How many need to protest, to write, to sing, to cry, to scream,
"Enough is enough!"
Questions without answers.
Answers without actions.

∞

I see an Earth reborn, free of humanity,
like the phoenix rising from the ashes,
a fertile planet, abundant with life,
no longer struggling to survive.

MOTHER EARTH - Our Shared Roots, AFRICA - The Cradle of Humanity, Acrylic on Canvas, ©Wendie Donabie.

Mother Earth Cries

Humankind stomps across our planet
leaving destruction in its wake.

Forests decimated,
species eradicated,
oceans and air polluted,
people starving,

dying,

dead.

Mother Earth cries.
"When will you ever learn, when will you ever learn?" [1]

Want trumps need, grows into greed.
More factories, more roads, more buildings.
More money, more of this, more of that.
We get what we want only to want more.
We have no joy in this wanting, in these gains.
We compete to have the most,
without concern for those who have less.

Our human nature wars against our humanity.

"When will you ever learn, when will you ever learn?"

"It took a pandemic to show you the way.
It took a lockdown to open your eyes.
But will your minds, your hearts and eyes cloud over again
once 'normal' days return?

Or will you see how I, Mother Nature,
can teach you to live,
to heal the planet.
Together, we can heal what you have harmed."

"When will you ever learn, when will you ever learn."

[1] Inspired by the Song, *Where Have All the Flowers Gone* by Pete Seeger. I changed 'we' in refrain to 'you'.

Avian Warnings

Last night, from my deepest dreams,
a covey of ravens gathered 'round.
Not the tricksters of legend and myth
but harbingers of what is to come.

They began with a cacophony of cackling croaks.
Then from somewhere within their midst,
a communal cry arose
that I knew I must attend.

In my dream I asked the ravens,
"Are you telling me there is still hope?"
With one powerful voice they replied,
"Indeed. You can make it so."

ON THIN ICE, Acrylic on Canvas, ©Wendie Donabie

WHISPERS OF SPRING, Acrylic on Canvas, ©Wendie Donabie

Whispers of Spring

Spring whispers to Mother Earth; spinning from season to season,

It's time for a wardrobe change.

She whispers to the sun, returning from her winter retreat,

It's time to awaken the sleeping earth, to melt away the last of winter.

She whispers to the wind, blowing last season's chill from the air,

It's time to sweep away the remnants of autumn, to prune trees of lifeless limbs.

She whispers to the trees, their lifeblood flowing once more,

It's time for your fresh green and nipple-red buds to burst into leaf.

She whispers to the birds, migrating to summer homes,

It's time to fill the Earth with song, to mate, to nest.

She whispers to the animals, rousing from long winter sleeps,

It's time to stir, to stretch your limbs, and greet the day again.

She whispers to the barn, birthing calves, colts, and piglets,

It's time to fling open your doors, to release your charges into the light.

She whispers to the farmer, preparing fields for seed,

It's time to sow, to bring forth fruits from the earth.

Spring whispers to humankind, yearning to break free from winter's icy clutches,

It's time for renewal, time to begin anew.

The Magic of Spring

My trembling hands reach out to touch the tender blossoms.
Soft, pearl-coloured, satin petals flutter in response.

Suddenly, a gust of wind shakes the branches,
raining down a flurry of flowers like a light winter's snow.

They swirl and twirl, performing calisthenic tricks
before blanketing the greening earth.

Such is spring — filled with fleeting magical moments,
with scenes of life awakening around us.

THE SAP IS RUNNING, Acrylic on Canvas, © Wendie Donabie

The Sap is Running

Mother Earth spins
welcoming spring in the north
where the sun warms slumbering maples
drawing their golden sap up, and down.

A childhood memory stirs —
Sunday drives on country roads
lined with maple trees,
pierced with spiles, adorned with silver pails.

And so, the ritual of spring begins again.
I wonder, if they feel pain
when the drill spins into their trunks
breaking through their gnarled bark.

I hope rather, they feel relief
from the pressure built up
before the sap begins to flow,
draining into waiting buckets.

I believe it's their gift to us,
some for more than two hundred years,
sharing their sweet nectar,
forgiving us for the wounds we inflict for our pleasure.

Watcher of the Spring

I watch,
quietly observing the return of spring.
Bird by bird, the days pass by towards summer.

Today grackles and blackbirds, traveling companions,
arrive from the south, blacken the snow,
in a feeding frenzy on and under bird feeders.

I listen.
Their cackles and shrill shrees,
cheerful chitters and tweets,
a cacophony of welcome chatter.

Naked trees,
Limbs tipped with reluctant buds,
fill with the noisy bird song,
I long to hear after winter's silent dearth.

CROCUS SURPRISE, Acrylic on Canvas Panel, ©Wendie Donabie

Crocus

What can be said of the lowly crocus,
harbinger of spring,
with its goblet shaped flowers
of dazzling white, fluorescent orange,
majestic purple, soft lilac.

This flirty flower, fertility symbol,
flourishes amongst blades of grass,
in collections of rocks,
in hollows of dead trees,
in our garden plots.

To our delight each spring
they push up through layers of leafy mulch
reaching for the sun,
and surprise us,
appearing in unexpected places,

their bulbs oft
replanted,
forgotten,
by critters
who squirreled them away.

TRILLIUM FANTASY, Watercolour on Paper, ©Wendie Donabie

Tricorn Hats

I stood at the start of the trailhead,
in awe of the forest below.
A carpet of white spread beneath the trees
wood lilies as far as my eyes could see.

Their three-petaled blossoms like tricorn hats
on an army of nuns on the march,
with reckless abandon surrounded the trees
their stunning beauty brought me to my knees.

I sat in silence to bask in the scene—
in a fortnight they would be gone.
Not a solitary sign of them would remain
'til next year when they'd bloom once again.

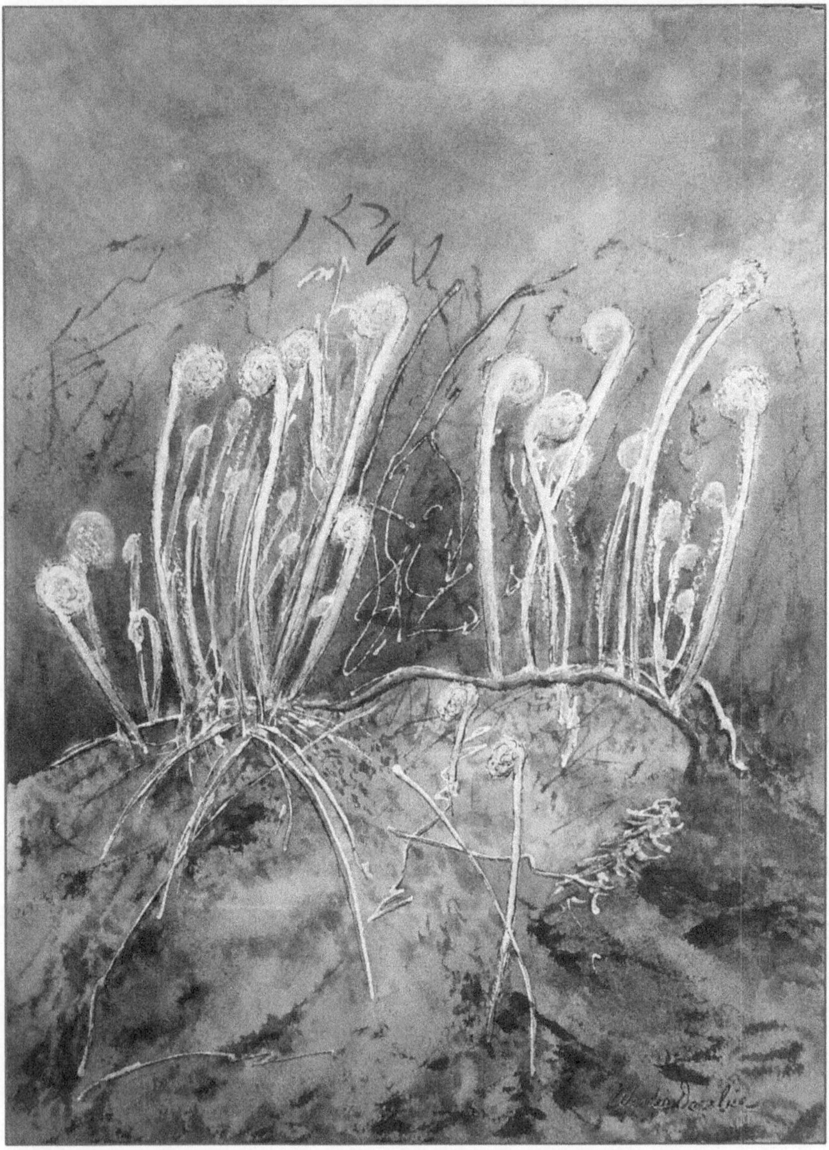

FIDDLEHEAD CONFLAB, Watercolour, Ink & Soft Pastel on Paper, ©Wendie Donabie

Aliens

Beneath the surface
alien creatures lie in wait,
moving like ninjas, silently in the dark,
ready to populate our forests and woodlots.

When spring warms the earth
they unfurl their leafy weaponry,
spiraling upwards into giant fronds,
expelling spores to propagate their kind.

They draw us in, with their luscious foliage.
We invite them to shade our gardens
and trust them to do no harm.

Are we being naïve?

DISCLAIMER: I love ferns

SUMMER AFTERNOON BY THE LAKE, Watercolour on Paper, ©Wendie Donabie

Summer Afternoon by the Lake

Heat shimmers off rippling sapphire waters

inviting me to plunge into their cool embrace.

Gentle waves softly kiss the shore.

Nearby a loon calls through the still, humid air,

a canoe comes into view,

a paddle rhythmically cuts the water with a gentle splash

on each lift.

This is a summer afternoon by the lake.

FLORAL BALLERINAS, Acrylic on Canvas, ©Wendie Donabie

Floral Ballerinas

Like prima ballerinas,

fuchsia tinted Coneflowers pose

against a backdrop

of emerald and olive greens.

Sporting multi-petalled tutus

and bright orange headdresses,

they provide stable landing pads

for buzzing bumble and honeybees.

Flitting from flower to flower

the ballet of bee and blossom begins

and a gentle breeze joins the performance,

travelling rhythmically across the garden stage

rousing the floral ballerinas to join in the dance,

their skirts aflutter.

WATERLILIES ON WOOD PADDLE, Acrylic, ©Wendie Donabie

MEDITATION – WATERLILIES ON CACHE LAKE, ALGONQUIN PARK, Acrylic on canvas, ©Wendie Donabie

Ode to the Water Lily

I envy you, water lily
quietly floating
along the shallow shore.

Your pearly white petals open
to welcome the day,
sunlight bursts forth
from your golden heart.

Like hands raised in varada mudra
you spread kindness,
emanating the peace
I so desperately seek.

STANDOUT, Acrylic on Canvas, ©Wendie Donabie

Stand Out

Despite entanglements

I press on.

Through the jungle of obstacles.

I push ahead.

Ever seeking the light

I stretch up.

Past rivals holding me down.

I reach forward.

Grappling for my place in the sun

I burst forth.

As a standout.

I bloom.

TOADSTOOLS & FIREFLIES, Watercolour on Paper, ©Wendie Donabie

Firefly Dating

Magic lives at night in the forest
as humans lie fast asleep
when fireflies gather to party
flashing lights for each other to see.

Seeking love in the dark isn't easy
But their lights help them find their next mate.
Much better than Match or eharmony
for beetles to set up a date.

To Listen is to Love

I spied two crows this morning
atop a barren oak.
One squawked and flapped incessantly,
the other never spoke.

He sat in stoic silence,
just listening to her speak.
When she was done he reached to her
and touched her beak to beak.

I stayed on there to watch them.
I thought what I could learn,
to listen far more often,
to love and not to spurn.

PATIENCE, Acrylic on Canvas, ©Wendie Donabie

Patience – Making Strides

Standing serene and patient,
mindful of all that surrounds you,
you teach us about waiting,
about vigilance,
about being watchful and alert.

You know yourself, Great Blue,
self reliant, resilient, and stable.
You take only what you need
and never more.
But that I would live like you.

I am making strides to know myself,
to understand as you do,
what is best for me,
to follow my heart,
and not my head.

SOARING, Oil on Canvas, ©Wendie Donabie

Soaring

Above the azure waters
along the granite shores
you soar with screeching, gurgling calls,
your feathers glistening white.

We watch your graceful swoops and dives
with envy in our hearts
to join you in your air ballet
to float above the Earth.

It is our dream to be like you,
to rise above our plights,
to lift on thermals in the sky
away from all our strife.

Today, defying gravity,
mankind has found a way
now born aloft on metal wings
subduing feet of clay.

BEAVER ON WOOD PADDLE, Acrylic, ©Wendie Donabie

On The Move

Do you ever rest, my beaver friend? All day you swim about gathering here and there more building materials, more décor for your abode, seeming an endless job.

You ply your trade from dusk to dawn, working your architectural magic, as lumberjack and carpenter. Cutting, chewing, dragging, pulling, swimming, climbing, weaving, straightening, mudding your palatial lodge.

Together, you and your special someone build your watery home, teach your young independents, industrious ways to keep a dwelling strong, safe, and secure.

Then when your days are done you can rest at last to slumber and dream of swimming, always swimming, on the move, into the dawn.

LOON ON WOOD PADDLE, Acrylic on Canvas, ©Wendie Donabie

Magical Moment

I heard your call before you appeared,
mystical bird of the north.
Your haunting, plaintive song
echoed across the placid lake.

Striking a regal pose, head held high,
in formal black and white attire,
your doppelgänger flawlessly mirrored in the water.

You called again, and your mate arrived.
Together you dove for dinner,
and I waited ... and waited
... and waited ...

Finally, you breached the surface,
reappearing next to me.
Your intense red eyes met my curious greens,
for a magical moment we connected.

Farewell to Summer

I wander through the forest bidding farewell
to the vibrant, lush greens of summer,
welcoming a fresh palette of corals, persimmons,
lemon yellows, fiery reds.

Before me the path lays littered
with a patterned quilt of auburn, gold, and ginger.
The only sounds, the crunch of leaves underfoot,
the honking of geese overhead.

In the crisp, sharp scent of autumn,
I inhale a hint of winter's breath
knowing soon this technicolour world
will transition to black and white, a time of rest.

The magic of nature
a continuous cycle of life —
ever changing,
from birth, through death to rebirth.

AUTUMN REFLECTION #1, Watercolour on Paper, ©Wendie Donabie

Autumn Reflection

It’s the shoulder season
when islands of amber grass dot the marshes
hillsides resplendent in rich jewel hues,
the crimson, coral, saffron gifts of autumn.

Summer residents gather
preparing a caravan to southern climes.
Their birdsong fills the air
as they bid us farewell.

Time for us to prepare
for the whitewash of winter;
to reflect on the fruitfulness
of seasons past and present.

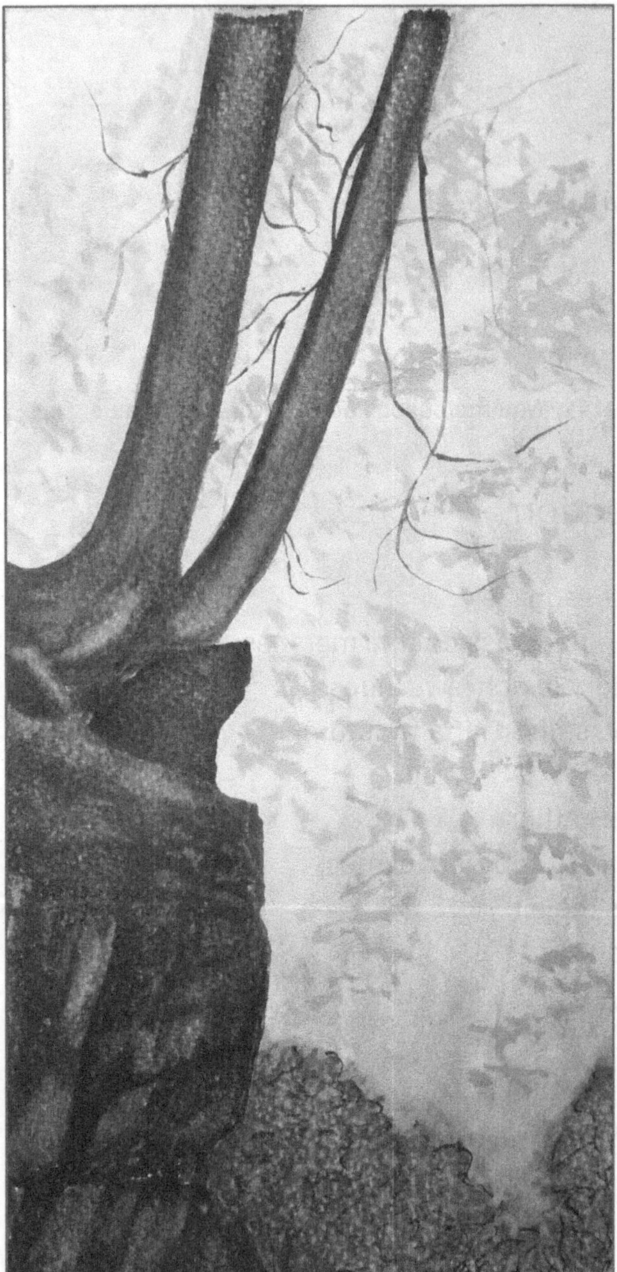

AUTUMN GOLD, Watercolour on Paper, ©Wendie Donabie

Gold

Some search for gold at rainbow's end,
a tale from days of old.
It's also found in autumn
when tree leaves turn to gold.

All that glitters is not gold,
or so the saying goes,
and though gold's incorruptible
man's nature is not so.

Gold is found in human hearts
when we cease our selfish deeds,
when our hearts guide us to act,
helping others fill their needs.

So. seek your gold in giving
or in autumn's rich display.
Though gold is incorruptible,
it can strip your soul away.

MEMORIES OF WALKS IN WINTER WOODS, Acrylic on Canvas,
©Wendie Donabie

Wendie Donabie

Winter Reflection

The first flakes of snow fell today.
Summer has fled,
and we wait
through the cold grey days of November
for the white brush strokes of winter,
its frosty bite is softened,
almost warmed,
by large flakes of slowly falling snow.

Walking in the woods on such days
feels like magic in the air.
Chickadees flit
from tree to tree.
Their happy chatter
filling the crisp air,
they land on my hand
if I bring them a treat.

Somewhere
in November's gloom
flashes of beauty occur
when the heavy clouds part
to reveal
the clear, peace-filled sky above.
Even in the darkest
of our days
there is light,
there is hope.

This is what we hang on to
what keeps us keeping on.

GATHERING IN WINTER, Chinese Ink on Paper, ©Wendie Donabie

Gathering in Winter

As winter storms blast and batter
and snow blankets your limbs and
climbs up your trunks,
you remain steadfast.

Perhaps you sleep
like bears, hibernating
'til those first warm rays of spring sun
touch your branches to awaken you.

Or is this time for you to commune
with your kin, sharing stories of summer,
of growth, of new life,
or of human decimation of your species.

WINTER FANTASY, Watercolour on Paper, ©Wendie Donabie

Frozen Forest

Winter wraps her ermine robes
‘round majestic pines and feathery firs
and carpets the forest floor
with a plush white cover
preparing for its long, deep slumber.

Through the silent woods
a dark brook winds,
its gurgling song
carrying with it
the stories of spring, summer, and fall.

The forest rests,
yet many creatures
still swoop amongst the branches,
tunnel through the deepening snow,
huddle together during the dark nights.

Winter's beauty lies in these still, quiet moments,
frozen in time,
free of conflict and strife.
Peaceful images of soft white hills
set against clear, cerulean skies.

Photo credit: ©Wendie Donabie

WINTER NOCTURNE, Acrylic on Canvas, ©Wendie Donabie

Homage to Frost: A Snowy Evening

A Glösa-style poem created using the first stanza of
Robert Frost's poem, *Stopping by Woods on a Snowy Evening*

I'm headed out into the snow.
A moonless night, as home I go.
Firs and pines all laden white;
whose woods these are? I think I know.

I muse this land belongs to Joe –
a man I've never cared to know.
He's never seen from year to year.
his house is in the village though.

Alone at night, I have no fear
that he might suddenly appear.
He'll be abed in his home now,
he will not see me stopping here.

I'll linger midst what trees here grow,
as feathery flakes blow to and fro.
He'll never know I paused tonight,
to watch his woods, fill up with snow.

The glosa is a poetic form with Spanish origins from the 15th century. A glosa typically consists of four ten-line stanzas each with ten syllables per line. The form also contains a borrowed excerpt from another writer. The borrowed quatrain, known as the cabeza, or "head," is presented at the beginning of the poem. Following this, each stanza expands upon one line of the cabeza while adhering to the rhyme scheme of ABBAACCDDC.
(Source: https://www.poetryfoundation.org/learn/glossary-terms/glosa)

Photo credit: Goldfinches on feeder, ©Wendie Donabie

NOTE: Native Americans see the Goldfinch as a symbol of unbridled joy, inspiration, motivation, and positivity. The song of the Goldfinch represents self-expression. In some tribes, it portends prosperity or liberation—the ability to be yourself without constraint.

Wings of Feathered Gold

Wings of feathered gold
flutter onto our feeder
like flickers of warm sunlight
bold against winter's white.

One, then two . . . four, then six
cling to the cylinder of food,
sing and peck the rich, black seed —
others perch above in wait.

Some jostle for a better position
but mostly they share in peace.

I never cease
to pleasure in their visits.

They return again and again
throughout the day
without fear of us spying
from our side of the glass.

Like summer heat pulsing
in each tiny, feathered frame
they set my heart aflame
on the coldest winter days.

FROZEN SHORELINE, Watercolour on Paper, ©Wendie Donabie

Winter Eye Candy

Ice covered rocks line the frozen shoreline —

odd-shaped confections topped with powdery, vanilla icing.

Branches span them hung with icicles of delicate sugar art.

Such winter eye candy can be found when we open our hearts and eyes.

SOLITUDE, Watercolour on Paper, ©Wendie Donabie

Winter Sabbatical

Silent, still, set apart,
biting winds whistling round,
snow gently drifting to blanket you,
insulating you from the world.

Your gate barred to predators,
those who would skin you,
ravage your structure
leaving you but bare bones.

Silent, still, set apart,
safe for another season,
only to end your sabbatical
with spring's return.

SPIRIT OF THE WINTER BARN, Watercolour on Paper, ©Wendie Donabie

Spirit of the Winter Barn

What haunts your vacant rafters
these cold midwinter nights
where swallows nested in the heat
and cattle lowed in stalls beneath?

I feel a presence living there —
a spirit watching over you,
a gentle, specter with no spite
who longs only to hold you tight.

So have no fear, dear winter barn,
I sense you're safe 'til spring returns.
Enjoy this quiet, peaceful pace
'til life fills up your empty space.

WINTER SOLSTICE, Watercolour on Paper, ©Wendie Donabie

Winter Solstice

Shut tight against winter's wrath, your boards creak in complaint.
Your stalls and silo crave summer's fill.
A blanket of sparkling snow drifts around you
protecting you through the long, bitter days
before the sun's return.

At Solstice you sense the coming warmth of summer,
small creatures stir in your darkest corners,
scurrying, seeking out scraps to sustain them
while doves coo a welcome
to the longer days.

WOODS IN WINTER, Acrylic Ink on Canvas, ©Wendie Donabie

Winter Wonder

Deep blue shadows speak of winter's sleep
as my boots crunch through crusty snow.
Chickadees and Blue Jays chatter and jeer from above
wondering at my presence.

I come for the white wonder of sparkling icy surfaces
where short days ago verdant green carpeted the forest floor
and canopy,
where boughs filled with birdsong,
and undergrowth with the skitter scattering of tiny feet.

I wonder at the miracle of everchanging life,
of this accidental place called Earth,
where every atom of creation has purpose,
where all existence belongs.

TREE OF LIFE, Watercolour on Paper,
©Wendie Donabie

Tree of Life

You came to me in vision
— a tree set apart in the woods.
Your blossoms held promise of abundant delights.
I yearned for your fruit, longing all day and night.

But then I remembered a similar tree
from a story writ long, long ago
of an apple that brought down paradise
and the woman blamed for making it so.

So, you will not tempt me to taste of your wares,
I'll struggle through life on my own,
by learning my lessons from choices I make,
and not blaming you for all my mistakes.

LIZ'S WOODPECKERED TREE, Watercolour on Paper, ©Wendie Donabie

Woodpeckered Tree

Over 50 years ago you stood proud,

arising from rocks, erect and full of life

yet time brought on the ravages of age.

You evolved into a host for creepy, crawly things,

a feast offered up for woodpeckers

who drilled your woody flesh and drained you of life.

Today you rest upon the waters,

waves lash you and strip away what bark remains,

yet you hang on, your roots held deep beneath the rocky shore.

This is tenacity, endurance, strength.

Against all odds, season after season, you remain an icon

to keep on going, no matter the challenges we face.

To Our Eastern Yellow Cedar

Deep rooted friend, standing so erect,
guardian of our home.

Your sweeping boughs laden with winter's frozen bounty
stretch out a fond embrace.

In summer months, your cooling shade
offers welcome respite.

All year long squirrels scurry up and down your feathery trunk.

Birds flee to your strong branches,
when danger nears.

Unaware of your vigilance,
little do they know you protect us too.

Firmly Rooted

Paths, crisscrossed
by gnarled, twisted roots,
and well-worn by tiny feet,
wound through maple and oak covered drumlins.

A colourama of seasons passed
from mint and emerald-green,
to ruby red, topaz orange,
sunlit gold, bronzed brown.

Days flew by
within the fortress
of those mystical woods
the stage of joy-filled, childhood play.

One ancient oak,
my stalwart guardian
stood silent outside my bedroom window,
its form silhouetted against the sheltering sky.

Today, those trees and I
still hold the land
with love,

firmly rooted.

DOUBLE ENTENDRE, Watercolour on Paper, ©Wendie Donabie

Double Entendre or Pas de Deux

Mirrored clouds dance upon the water
in rhythm with their sky-born twins,
performing a symmetrical ballet
Tchaikovsky would awe.

A grounded gathering of willow and pine
line the shore,
their reflections joining the choreography.
swaying in time with the repertoire.

Whispering winds and lapping waves,
in accompaniment,
offer an orchestral arrangement,
unmatched by human skill.

WILSON FALLS, BRACEBRIDGE, Watercolour on Paper, ©Wendie Donabie

Escape

Haiku

Tumbling falls descend
Still forests rise to greet me.
Here in my escape.

WELCOMING WOODS, Acrylic on Canvas, ©Wendie Donabie

Forest Bathing

The forest beckons me to wander
and weave my way
through paths of sun speckled, twisted roots
and sheltering limbs.

A raven's shrill call invites me
deeper,
deeper,
into his sacred space.

I settle
on the stump of an ancient oak,
its rings of life still solid, strong.

I close my eyes.
Whispering boughs rustle overhead,
a gentle breeze kisses my cheek.

I inhale
the musty odour of rich, moist earth,
and the crisp, fresh, scent of pine.

My heart slows,
beating in unison
with the rhythms of the forest.

Like a drop of rain
falling into a flowing river
I release myself to the multiverse.

I feel
the shackles of my singular being
drop away.

I free float, unrestrained
in a sea of tranquility
to the song of the cosmos.

I sense
no beginnings, no endings—
I'm a part of all creation.

Time and space
have no meaning here—
concepts only of the mind.

Then, like the chime of a singing bowl,
the raven's call draws me back.
I leave the forest renewed.

OUT OF THE WOODS, Acrylic on Canvas, ©Wendie Donabie

GATHERING OF ELDERS, Chinese Ink on Paper, ©Wendie Donabie

Wendie Donabie

Gathering of Elders

I heard their whispers, as I passed,
in throaty, deep, and resonant tones.
They spoke of mankind's lack of care,
of genocide and lands stripped bare.

So many species gone for good,
could we not see the harm we caused?
I sensed their sorrow, the searing pain
of generations lost in vain.

They called on me to share their plight,
to leave their fate to nature's will
then they'd adapt and truly thrive
and help all life on Earth revive.

I made a vow to them that day
with hand upon the tallest tree,
"I'll change my ways to help regain
and reestablish nature's reign."

TWILIGHT RIDGE, Chinese & Acrylic Inks on Paper, ©Wendie Donabie

Dream

Silent sentinels,
you cling to ancient rocks,
reach to the endless sky.
Your gnarled and twisted roots
bind you to this place.

Like rockets set to launch,
you stretch up to the stars,
fast tethered to the Earth.
Do you dream of release,
of escape into space?

TREE AT REST, Watercolour on Paper, ©Wendie Donabie

The Pose

I met you in the woods one day,

rising high above me,

quietly resting in a relaxed pose against a rocky mound,

rooted ankles crossed.

It was that pose that captured my eye,

so much like my cat, Amber.

She often found a sunlit spot, warmth caressing her,

eyes shut tight with her paws crossed.

I felt I knew you in that moment,

both of us part of creation

made of the same material

meant to live as family, in harmony.

CONTENTMENT, Chinese Ink on Paper, ©Wendie Donabie

Inspired by this quote by John Muir:

"I never saw a discontented tree. They grip the ground as though they liked it, and though fast rooted they travel about as far as we do. They go wandering forth in all directions with every wind, going and coming like ourselves, traveling with us around the sun two million miles a day, and through space heaven knows how fast and far!"

The Contentment of Trees

Tall and silent, towering over me,
branches spread wide,
tenderly intertwining
with your forest companion's
like lovers holding hands.

Your roots journey out
beyond your canopy,
cross my path,
then dive beneath the surface,
meeting with others traveling there.

Here in natures' cathedral
you live together in harmony,
peacefully communing,
all species fulfilling their calling,
without our interference.

ALONG SPRUCE BOG TRAIL, ALGONQUIN PARK, Acrylic on Canvas, ©Wendie Donabie

Castle Keep

Beneath my feet pine straw yields,
a scent so fresh and clean.
The day both crisp and sunlit,
as we hike this forest scene.

From walls of granite boulders
woodland creatures hide and peep,
keeping close watch o'er their realm,
high within their castle keep.

They track our route along the path
ensuring we're not here to stay.
We hear them chatter in the leaves
as if to say, "Be on your way."

MOONLIT WOODS, Acrylic Ink on Canvas, ©Wendie Donabie

Deep in the Woods

The darkness wraps me like a cloak,
deep in the woods tonight,
where creatures fly and stalk about
in shadows birthed by moonlight.

The chattering creek shares stories,
magic tales from ancient times,
of faeries, elves, and sprites
who aided all mankind.

Those fae creatures bide today
beneath the woodland knolls.
We can always call on them
to help our troubled souls.

WOODLANDS CYLE OF LIFE – MOSS COVERED STUMP,
Watercolour & Soft Pastel on Paper, ©Wendie Donabie

Recycling

In Mother Nature's hands
the forest recycles.
Nothing is wasted.

A tree dies and decays to feed and nourish new life.
Mosses, lichen, and fungi erupt,
and disperse over the stump,
insects dig and drill,
all thriving on the rotting wood.

Birds, wind, and forest creatures deposit seeds
in a mulch of leaves and mouldering trees.
Rich nutrients feed them, the sun warms them,
they germinate, seedlings emerge.

The cycle begins anew.

TRULY MUSKOKA, Acrylic on Canvas, ©Wendie Donabie)

It Will Travel On

*a Nonet Poem

A broad navy ribbon threads its way

through rich, emerald-green forests

bearing stories to the sea

of lands, lakes, beasts, and man.

It will travel on

when we have gone.

Earth can thrive

without

us.

* A nonet is a nine-line poem. In the nonet form, each line contains specific, descending syllable counts. The first line contains nine syllables, the second line contains eight, and the third line contains seven, and so on. The last line of nonet poetry contains one syllable.

CROWNING GLORY, Acrylic on Canvas, ©Wendie Donabie

Crowning Glory

While wandering a woodland path, I happened to view a pearly-white crown atop a sturdy stem standing erect high above the forest floor.

Held securely in the crook of a broken limb, the tree itself chose to provide a throne for its alien companion.

Was this regal mushroom holding court for the fruitful fungi below, living amidst deadfall and debris?

I will never know this saprophyte's story, yet I could weave magical tales as tangled as the mycelium mother from which it sprang.

Stories of mushroom kingdoms and toadstool knights arising from a dark underground world bringing both destruction and benefit.

Such inspiring surprises await the sharp-eyed hiker, like
treasures hidden in plain sight,
rewards for our hungry imaginations.

'SHROOMS ON THE ROCKS AT CACHE LAKE GENERAL STORE, ALGONQUIN PARK, Acrylic on Canvas, ©Wendie Donabie

'Shrooms on the Rocks

With your spongy caps and feathered gills
I wonder at times if you are perhaps more related to a
subterranean species of fish living in the ground,
popping up here and there for air.

But the truth of your life is far more extraordinary.
Miles and miles of mycelium nourish you
until you are mature
and ready to reproduce.

You emerge from the earth, from decaying tree stumps,
amongst clusters of rocks
to spread your spores
and continue the life cycle of your kind.

Neither plant, nor animal, you stand alone as a species,
lacking the ability to photosynthesize,
you secrete enzymes to absorb nutrition from your
surroundings.

We can learn so much from you—
how you sense and adapt to environmental signals,
changing your development, direction of growth, and
metabolism.

I wonder then if you were sent as a gift
from an alien race
who knew we would need your wisdom
when we began to wipe out life here on Earth.

Photo credit: ©Wendie Donabie

THREE TOXIC REDHEADS, Soft Pastel on Paper, ©Wendie Donabie

Three Toxic Redheads

Wandering through the forest deep,
you spy their bright red domes.
Their pretty heads catch your eye,
tempting you to take them home.

That red should be a warning
to stop before you pick.
Their flesh contains a toxin
to make you very sick.

Often seen in fairy tales
an exquisite fungus to view,
you'd not expect this lifeform,
could cause serious harm to you.

WHELK SHELL, Watercolour on Paper, ©Wendie Donabie

Seashell Soliloquy

As a young child, I recall
receiving an Atlantic Whelk shell.
“Put it up to your ear,” I was told.
And I heard the ocean roar.

My eyes lit up with excitement
and my love of the sea began,
or perhaps it was rekindled.
That is the mystery!

* * * * * * * * * * * * * * * * **

Photo credit: ©Wendie Donabie

Today, I mudlark on seashores
building a treasure trove of magical, mollusk shells,
the ocean giant's generous gifts
found strewn on the sand when tides recede.

Waves wash over the powdery beach,
I'm lulled by the ocean's heartbeat.
I inhale its fishy scent,
taste saltiness on my tongue.

Screeches and squawks of sea birds grow,
perhaps warning me away,
as they come to dine
on a fresh feast of cockles, clams, mussels and more.

Gulls, terns, oystercatchers,
sanderlings, and their kin,
race for those delectable delicacies
delivered by the briny deep.

They skitter along the beach,
taking flight if I draw too near.
But my focus is not on them—
it's on what they leave behind.

Astonishing specimens,
from Conchs to Clams and Coquinas
each a vacant, discarded home,
distinct in size and shape.

Like handcrafted sculptures
their fine detailed swirls and ridges,
spirals and open cups of iridescence,
still seem to pulse with life.

Individual marks and shading,
colours covering the spectrum —
foam white to squid ink black,

ultramarine to pearlescent pink.
What is their allure,
drawing me to dig my toes into the warm sand,
eyes focused,
scanning the beach for my next prize?

Is it simply the ebb and flow
within me —
a biological response
to the moon and the tides?

Am I reconnecting with my life in the womb
where I began my human journey,
free floating my first nine months
in a tiny fetal sea?

Could it be my reptilian brain,
driving this keepsake obsession,
recalling our primordial origins,
our primeval departure from the sea?

I buy bijouterie
created from shells,
wear them as totems
to the ocean, our distant past.

Like a loved one's ashes
I save them as ancestral relics,
the scent of the sea lingering
in shell-filled jars and bowls.

At home amid my treasures
I hear surf breaking on the shore,
gulls calling overhead –

the sea in me restored.

Photo credit: ©Wendie Donabie

Photo credit: ©Wendie Donabie, Sand Crab, Veradero, Cuba

Sand Crabs

It’s the skittering shadow I see first,

then the spindly legs.

And when the movement stops,

it’s those two black, beady eyes

perched above the shiny, shell body,

staring right at me

that freaks me out!

Dawn's First Light

In dawn's first light,
the blanket of the sea
sparkles like a tray of diamond dust
and from beneath his watery coverlet,
the ocean giant rolls over,
defying wakefulness.

Floating birds tossed into the air
drift down and settle again
to ride the steady rise and fall
of his deep, full breath,
while along the beach,
sandpipers chatter after the retreating surf
snatching up breakfast morsels.

Gulls nesting on the sand
reluctantly lift heads from downy warmth,
blink at the rising sun,
stand and stretch,
voices screeching complaints of dawn's too early arrival,
then soar, silver-winged into the light.

Turning of the Tide

The briny river ebbs
with the tide,
slowing to a moment
of mirrored calm.

Shellfish blowholes
speckle the shore—
pancakes,
ready to be turned.

Skirting the water's edge,
plovers stop and spear the sand
for a quick snack.

A macho mallard
proudly escorts his lady
to the riverside,
for a leisurely lunch
at the strand.

Once sated,
the diners linger,
unaware of their host's endless plight,
as seabound to deliverance,
the current is halted,
turned back,
denied freedom once more.

With belly refilled
to feed its patrons,
the captive river rushes upstream
more quickly it seems
then it left.

Still indentured
to an unseen master,
it waits,
building momentum
for the next turning of the tide.

Photo credit: ©Wendie Donabie

Photo credit: ©Wendie Donabie

TIME TOGETHER, Watercolour, Soft Pastel & Ink on Paper,
©Wendie Donabie

Daybreak at Cape Cod

Leaning corpse-cold
against each other,

we wait.

Lingering night shivers over us,
the eastern sky still shut tight
against the leaden sea.

We watch

whispering waves sweep the cluttered beach
washing away the debris of yesterday.

Silent,

still,

we stand

silhouetted against the breaching dawn.

Photo credit: ©Wendie Donabie

The Lure of the Sea

I am lured to the seaside
by Thalassa, goddess of the ocean,
attuned to her heartbeat,
the steady rise and fall of her watery surge.

She calls me to be near her,
to step away from the busyness of life,
to commune with the sea in me,
to simply breathe in this moment.

In the distance, the surf crescendos
to a mighty roar
quieting to pianissimo
as it reaches the shore.

Waves trimmed with crocheted foam
dance rhythmically along the warm sand,
while seabirds glide above me
declaring their dominion over the waters below.

I cannot fly in the air
or live in the sea.
yet the briny scent beckons me
to this place that feels like home.

Photo credit: ©Wendie Donabie. Oyster Catchers on Anna Maria Island, Manatee County, Florida

Seascape

Navy satin
lines the bay beyond my window,
where white sails fly
and black seals
come to court in spring.

Rounded pyramids of pitch pine
border the shore,

giving rise to birch —
white-faced geishas bowing genteelly
to the passing fleet of fair-weather sailors.

From every walk of life,
birds flutter,
glide,
flap by,
caw,
screech,
squawk,
their coded communiqués.

While,
beneath the sea,
unseen,
life goes on as usual.

And I,
from my window bay,
am witness to this moving seascape,
framed by my contentment.

Photo credit: ©Wendie Donabie. Fin/Finback Whale calf

Whale Watch (Rye, New Hampshire)

The rolling ship
tracks oily footprints to our prey,
as chattering dolphins,
offer running commentary on the voyage,
and the pungent smell of ocean spray,
lies wet upon my face.

Eyes alert,
on bated breath I await
my first sighting.
Suddenly, someone yells,
“There she blows!”
I rush to the rail.

Two spouts of white mist shoot skyward,
one giant, one smaller fluke follows,
as the ocean giants dive again.
The ship adjusts her heading,
soon side by side, we swim together.

Sixty-foot-long Finback Whale,
her half-size baby, and man —
all sociable creatures
sharing an afternoon on the sea.

Mother whale knows the Granite State,
by her sound.
She feels secure,
and leaves the ship and passengers to calf-sit,
while she lunches, just within our sights.

In his watery playpen
baby rolls over,
shows his white belly,
grins and dives beneath us,
again, and again.

Tons of ballistic grace
race us and chase us,
neither playmate tiring
of this magical game of hide and seek.

Then without warning,
he heads straight out to sea.
Lunch finished,
his mother calls,
his fluke waves farewell.

GENESIS, Acrylic on Canvas, 24 x 30 inches, Mother Humpback Whale & Calf, ©Wendie Donabie

Season's End

Windward blows
sweep across deserted lawns,
through empty porches,
pummelling window sashes,
cleaning out the last of summer's guests.

Facing out to sea,
the spirits of lost sailors' wives
haunt rope rockers.
Back and forth they creak,
awaiting their mates' return.

Ripples grow to breakers,
whispered lappings rise
to a quiet roar
of eternal fidelity,
as autumn brings tall ghostly ships.

Sailors' wives and other lovers greet
and within the quiet,
empty spaces
left at season's end,
silent laughter rings.

SEASIDE REVERIE, Acrylic on Canvas, ©Wendie Donabie

Sea Reverie

From my landlocked northern home,
waves of nostalgia
carry me back to the sea,

where in the black of moonless nights,
the sky and sea are one.
Stars high above reflect as countless points of light
upon the waters below,

and like a mighty panther,
the ocean purrs contentedly,
lulling me to sleep,
to dream of days by the sea.

Dawn's Kiss

The first rays of dawn
tiptoe
across the dew dropped grass
and leap
into my window,
flit across the polished floor,
slink over silken sheets,
and kiss
my face.

I relish such mornings,
like fresh bread and honey,
soft to chew and sweet on the tongue.

Light delights me as it plays through the day,
changing the mood of each place it touches.

Sunrise

Sleep-filled eyes gaze at the blazing sun
flashing hot hues 'tween earth and sky.
Brilliant colours transform,
to a muted rainbow,
as the golden orb
rises higher
heading west
seeking
rest.

Photo credit: ©Wendie Donabie

RIVER OF HEAVEN, Acrylic on canvas, ©Wendie Donabie

River of Heaven

On those darkest of nights
your brilliance stretches over us,
glittering points of light
clutched within your celestial grip.

We who fear the dark, close our eyes,
yet here is where you shine the brightest.
In the dark you show us the possibilities
that light obscures.

We who do not fear the dark
are drawn to you,
seekers, adventurers, explorers,
finding truths to share in the light.

As night moves into day,
you travel on
your endless journey
always returning to remind us.

There is always hope.

There is always a way.

Chinese Ink on Paper, ©Wendie Donabie

Moon Dance

Moonlight floods the tree-lined shore

as cosmic strains

pulse with rhythms

setting Jack Pines to sway.

They bow to approaching waves,

issuing an invitation to dance.

Together they waltz to celestial music

only they can hear.

MOON DANCE,

The Moon

I fall into a swoon
at the sight of the moon
like a romantic tune
or the call of a loon.

Though singers will croon
about love coming soon
of the Strawberry moon
appearing in June,

at night I cocoon
at home in my woon*
and commune with the moon
my life to attune.

*Woon definition: domicile, residence, home, abode (place of living), residence.

STAY ROOTED WHILE REACHING FOR THE STARS,
Acrylic on Canvas, ©Wendie Donabie

Stay Rooted While Reaching for the Stars

Endless space, vacuum of hydrogen and helium
the elements of life
dark energy, infinite black holes.

Home to hot, burning stars, spinning galaxies,
shooting comets, undiscovered planets,
vast, unchartered vistas to explore —
man's footloose fantasy— free of earthly roots.

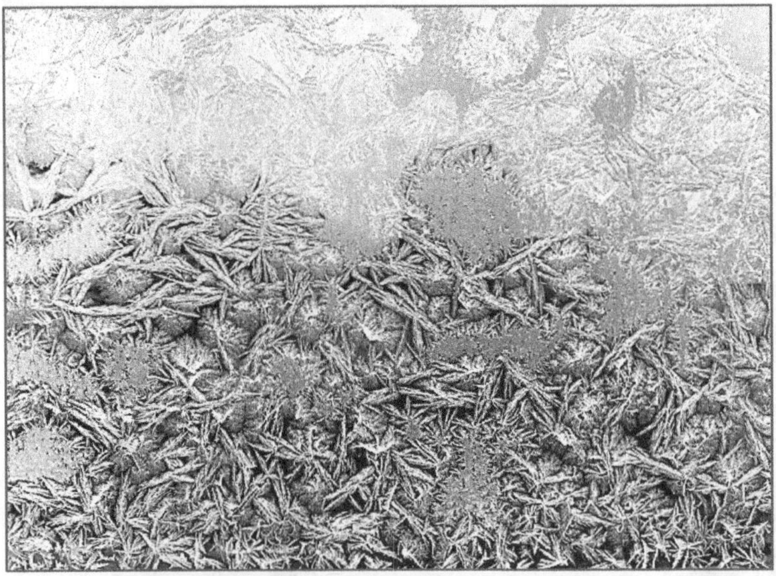

Photo credit: ©Wendie Donabie. Winter frost on window

Through Frosted Glass

What frigid thoughts travel through the minds of humans,
who slaughter and control without mercy,
who devastate the air, land, and sea?

I'm chilled to the bone by the violent, ruinous images,
and haunting, horrific sounds
filling both screen and print,

as I view the world through frosted glass
hiding from those who are suffering,
feeling powerless to help.

FIELD OF REMEMBRANCE, Acrylic on Canvas, ©Wendie Donabie

Where Poppies Grow

In fields of crosses, poppies grow,
spawned by the blood of men.
The cost of victory stained the flower
when war came to an end.

They grow as silent sentinels
to those who fought and died
preserving freedom for a world
where lust for power abides.

FRUIT OF THE VINE, Watercolour on Paper, ©Wendie Donabie

Hope

We cling to hope
like a vine holds fast to a wire fence,
secure,
it grows and winds along the path laid before it.

Believing it will always be there,
we too look for signs and guideposts to lead us,
needing to trust and rely on our decisions,
unable to see clearly what lies ahead.

Then the wire breaks,
and like the vine
we must reach for a new handhold,
find a new path.

Once again we cling to hope
that our choices are the right ones

ROCK, PAPER, SCISSORS – A NATURAL COLLABORATION,
Mixed Media on Canvas, ©Wendie Donabie

Rock, Paper, Scissors

They challenged us.
Rock, Paper, Scissors,
a game of competition,
create an art piece with this theme.

Being one who dislikes competition,
and the oft arising conflict,
I worked out a way
to unify these disparate parts.

Scissors formed trees.
Stones became rocks.
Paper created ground texture,
and paint detailed and unified the whole.

Are we capable of rewriting our conflicts in this way?

Can love and acceptance provide the paint,
and our actions be the brushes
to unify us,
to bring all people together?

WHAT ONCE WAS HOME, Acrylic on Canvas, ©Wendie Donabie

What Once Was Home

She sinks below the tall, wild grasses,
her withered, weather worn bones leaning
from years of snow and rain;
she groans as winds whistle through her empty shell.

Time has punched holes in the cedar-shingled roof
that once crowned her sturdy frame,
stripped away her doors and windows,
leaving gaping holes inviting the outside in.

Yet, those who loved her linger on —
guardians of her past,
they watch,
as nature feasts upon their memories.

Vines spread over her failing form
covering her with a shroud of vibrant green.
She knows her days are numbered,
but in her place, life will carry on.

Photo credit: ©Wendie Donabie, Abandoned house

REFLECTION, Watercolour on Paper, ©Wendie Donabie

Reflection

As my kitchen window reflects my neighbour's home,
so, I see myself in you.
What I like and love about you, I like and love about myself.
What I judge about you, I judge about myself.

If I'm angered by your words or actions,
I'm angered by my own.
I see in you what I criticize in myself —
what makes me frustrated, frightened,
annoyed, sad.

You show me all of who I am —
my flaws and my beauty marks.

Recognizing our differences
and how we are the same
is how we learn acceptance,
how we come together.

To grow, to reconcile, to heal,
to build community,
to become whole.

VISION QUEST, Acrylic and Chinese Ink on Watercolour Paper,
©Wendie Donabie

Vision Quest

He was of the age to seek his purpose
as he set out in the dark.

Deep in the woods he made camp
by a moonlit waterfall
not knowing what would transpire.

And the elders gathered 'round.

Demons and angels warred in his sleep
as he wrestled with himself
his body drenched in sweat.

In his dreams, his family, his community
stood silent watching, waiting,
wondering who would return to them.

And the elders gathered 'round.

In the night he awoke to a rustling in the brush
and a gruff voice spoke,
"Your courage will make you
a great leader. I will be with you."

And the elders gathered 'round.

From the dark, a towering, black bear emerged,
reared up, met his gaze,
and ambled away.

And the elders gathered 'round.

PEOPLE OF THE SUNFLOWER, Acrylic on Canvas, ©Wendie Donabie.
Painted in response to Russia's attack on Ukraine on February 24, 2022.

People of the Sunflower

(Helianthus Populus)

(for the people of Ukraine)

Brave faces turn to the sun,
stand strong, unmoved,
against attack.

Seeds of loyalty and pride
planted in their hearts
draw them together.

Roots hold firm
in rich, fertile soil
defying any adversary

This is the soul of Ukraine.
This is the power of its people.
This is their fight for freedom.

SUNFLOWER, graphite sketch, ©Wendie Donabie

Hope

In the space,

between the pavement

and the bomb-levelled home,

the oak tree clung to life,
its limbs splintered
by shrapnel.

Beside it a solitary sunflower
its face bent in sorrow
looked down at a wine glass,

shattered.

Nature grieves for us,

yet hopes,

for an end to war.

We are One

"Everything sooner or later is part of everything else."

– Mary Oliver, *Poem of One World*

Yes, Mary,

I agree.

there is comfort in this thought,

and beauty in acknowledging

we are not superior or lesser than anything else that exists.

We are part of everything that exists —

part of each ant that scurries about doing ant things,

each leaf blowing in the wind,

all creatures in the air, in the sea, on the land,

every person living in the farthest reaches of the Earth.

If I Knew Magic

If I knew a healing spell,
or could concoct a potion,
my magic might well save the Earth—
that is my hopeful notion.

Enchantments would change humankind
who choose to do their worst,
to destroy and lay to waste.
Their selfish wishes coming first.

We've become so arrogant
and filled with boundless greed,
driving us to mindless acts
taking far more than we need.

We've overbred the planet,
polluted air and water
deforested and strip-mined,
and caused a wildlife slaughter.

And now with global warming,
we've very few more years
to stabilize the ozone
as our Doomsday fast draws near.

Cut out the power politics —
they've no place in this fight.
Allied, we all can save our home,
to restore and put things right.

There's real magic we can do
with human imagination
to preserve our planet now
through world collaboration.

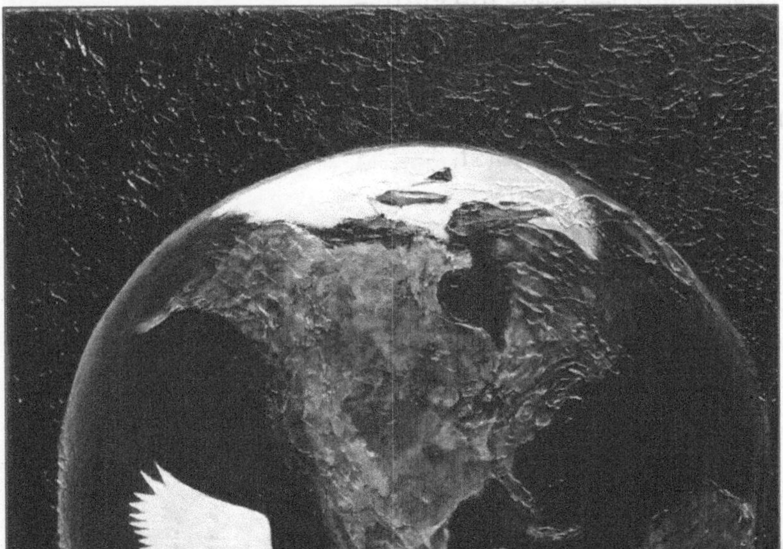

IMAGINE, Acrylic on Canvas, ©Wendie Donabie

BREATH OF LIFE, Acrylic on Canvas, ©Wendie Donabie
(The Earth held in a tree's embrace)

Read about the importance and benefits of trees
https://treecanada.ca/resources/benefits-of-trees/

BREATH OF LIFE, acrylic on Canvas, ©Wendie Donati [illegible]
[illegible] Earth held in a tree's embrace [illegible]

[illegible]

Thanks & Acknowledgements

To the Baysville Writing Group, I offer my heartfelt appreciation for listening to my work and encouraging me as a writer.

Kudos and a tip of my pen to my talented critique group partners, Cindy Watson, Lori Knowles, Sherry Rondeau, and Paul Feist, for critiquing each poem, recommending ways to lay out this book, supporting my writing efforts and providing a proverbial 'kick in the ass' when needed, and to prolific poet, David Bruce Patterson, a special thanks for his poet's viewpoint and edits. The book would not have happened without your encouragement.

To the members of our Publishing Roundtable group, (the critique members listed above plus Nancy Beal, Bev Brewer, and Kaitlyn Sutey), thank you for sharing your writing and publishing insights. Your experiences helped me avoid many bumps on my way to publication.

My deep appreciation to my dear friend, Carolyn Freedman, and friend and fellow writer, Aviva Derenowski, for reading my work and providing critical input. And thanks to Mary Lou Ingham for her reader's eagle eyes!

Lastly, my love and gratitude to my extraordinary life partner, Hugh Nichols, who believes in me, supports all my artistic ventures, constantly inspires me, and whose love keeps me going on those days when I feel the creative well might run dry.

About the Author

Wendie Donabie's poetry and short prose have been published in magazines and in literary anthologies. *Mother Earth, The Mother of Us All,* included in this collection won gold in Art Ascent Magazine in 2014.

Views from the Edge of the Earth is her debut collection. Some pieces are birthed from her paintings; others sparked by life experiences.

Wendie is an active member of Muskoka Authors Association, cofounded with Cindy Watson in 2015. She is also a painter with a small gallery (Heron's Nest Studio Gallery) in her home where she carries her paintings along with work by other local artists.

In 2010, Wendie moved to majestic Muskoka where she lives with her life partner and strongest supporter, Hugh Nichols.

Wendie would love to hear your thoughts about *Views from the Edge of the Earth* and about what we can do to help the planet.

You can write to Wendie at info@wendiedonabie.com. Or visit her at Heron's Nest Studio Gallery, 95 Muskoka Road, Bracebridge, Ontario.